One-Minute

Developmental Drill
Level B Division
Divisors 6 to 9

Grades 6-9

by
Theresa Warnick

Frank Schaffer
An imprint of Carson-Dellosa Publishing LLC
Greensboro, North Carolina

DIRECTIONS FOR USE

Setting up the Program

Reproduce enough copies of the tests for the class. You may wish to separate the tests by fact into file folders and organize the folders in a storage box. This provides handy access to the tests and a quick view of the pages which need to be replenished. Using a manila file folder for each student offers easy organization and provides a simple method of distributing the daily tests.

Using the Flash Cards

A set of flash cards is required for each student. These serve as additional facilitators in learning and retaining basic math facts.

Included in this book is one set of flash cards for divisors six to twelve. The flash cards for divisors six to nine follow the sequence found on the teacher and student progress charts. For enrichment activities, the flash cards displaying divisors ten to twelve are also included in the set.

When beginning the program, give each student only those facts he or she has mastered on the progress chart and the first unchecked fact. This card will correspond to the test the student will be taking. Each time another fact is mastered, give the student the card for the next fact. Unmastered flash cards may be left in the student's folder for easy access.

Encourage the use of the flash cards at home as well as at school. Depending on the number of cards being reviewed, you may wish to spend five to fifteen minutes a day on flash card practice.

Using the Bulletin Board

The "Some Cool Math Facts!" bulletin board theme can be used to highlight the particular facts on which students are working. Using the reproducible art found on page vi write the math facts on the icebergs, whale, polar bear, and seal. You may enlarge the reproducible illustrations for the bulletin board by using the opaque projector or by making a transparency of the illustrations in order to use the overhead projector.

Using the Progress Charts

The progress chart shows the division facts and indicates the scope and sequence of Level B (divisors six to nine). By checking off each fact a student masters, you can record each student's progress. Each student may track his or her own progress by coloring a copy of the personal progress charts found on pages x and xi.

The Letter to Parents

The letter provided will help make parents aware of the objectives, components and methods of the **One-Minute Math Developmental Drill** series.

Awards and Certificate of Achievement

When a student completes a designated number of facts, you may wish to present him or her with an award found on page ix. The certificate may be used when all of the facts in the Level B Division are mastered.

Using the Manipulative Mats

It is important that students develop a good understanding of numbers. The following activities will help students create relations for numbers and will help strengthen their number sense.

Have the students work with a variety of materials on the manipulative mat (page viii). These mats may be laminated for extended use.

1. Select a number of counters representing dividends for divisors six to nine. If, for example, the selected dividend is eighteen and the divisor is six, the student may separate the counters on the mat into six groups of three counters. Next, the student should verbalize the parts shown, for example: "Eighteen divided by six equals three." Allow the students adequate practice in manipulating the counters on the mat into sets for other dividends and divisors. (See illustration A.)

A

2. Select a dividend and ask the students to place the correct number of counters on their mats. Have the students write that number at the top of blank sheets of paper. Students should use their counters to find all the possible divisors for the selected dividend and record the division sentences. (See illustration B.)

B

Using the Game Sheet

Game Sheet (page viii): Fill in the blank spaces on the path with the number facts you wish to reinforce. Some students may be interested in decorating the game sheet with markers or crayons and giving the game a title. The game sheet may be laminated for extended use. Using a gameboard spinner, the student moves ahead the number of spaces shown and must correctly answer the number fact to remain on that space. If the correct answer is given, the next player may take a turn. If the student answers incorrectly, he or she returns to the previously held space.

The game may end when one player reaches the final space on the path or it may continue until all players reach the end space. Students may also play in teams. The first students to complete the game sheet may fill in the facts for the next game to be played.

Using the Timed Tests

Level B Division teaches divisors six to nine. Each sheet contains 30 problems. There is a pretest and posttest for placement and evaluation. The particular fact the student is learning appears 40% of the time (twelve problems) on each test. The last previous fact mastered occurs 10% to 20% of the time (three to six problems). The remaining 40% to 50% of the problems on each sheet are those previously learned by the student, except for those pages labeled as tests, which usually present each fact only once. Each sequence of facts, such as the dividing by six, ends with a test just focusing on those facts. This test can be used as a diagnostic tool to pinpoint particular sequences of facts not known. For instance, a student may already know the quotients when dividing by six, but not know the answers when dividing by seven. These section tests may help to assess this. Students using the program should also take these section tests when appropriate.

Each student should complete a timed test every day if possible, starting with the lowest fact on the progress chart for that student. Remind the students to note the fact written in the upper lefthand corner, which indicates the fact on which they are working. Students must complete all the problems on a sheet accurately **in one minute** before advancing to the next fact. If the student has not completely and accurately answered all the problems when the minute has elapsed, he or she must complete a test for the same fact the next day. If students have extreme difficulty passing each fact page, you may wish to lengthen the amount of time allowed to complete the page by five or ten seconds.

It is important to allow students to see their progress on the same fact. All attempted tests may be left in the folder and the same fact test added on top for the next day. Students will become more proficient each time they are retested on the same fact until they finally master it.

Not all students will complete the entire program, but they will possess a greater proficiency of the facts they have mastered. Mastery, rather than completion, is the goal of the program.

Dear Parent,

In order to develop a good mathematics foundation, it is important that your child learns basic multiplication and division facts. The **One-Minute Math Developmental Drill** program enables children to achieve this goal. The idea behind this program is for children to master a particular math fact before they are introduced to a new fact.

A flash card will be sent home each time your child begins learning a new division fact. The flash cards will help your child memorize these facts more readily. Please have your child practice daily with **all** of the flash cards you have received. He or she should work toward answering each card in less than two seconds. Help your child with this activity if possible. Since it may take several days to commit some facts to memory, be patient with your child. Children will not learn all facts at the same rate. Do not expect your child to bring home a new flash card every day.

The Level B Division program includes:

1. Placement test, pretest and posttest for placement and evaluation

2. 44 individual fact tests on divisors six to nine

   a. Each test contains 30 problems.

   b. The particular fact a student is learning is covered in 40% of the test.

   c. The previously learned fact is covered in 10% to 20% of the test.

3. 40 flash cards for practicing the selected facts

4. Certificate of completion and awards.

Thank you for working with me on this program.

Please contact me if you have any questions or concerns.

Sincerely,

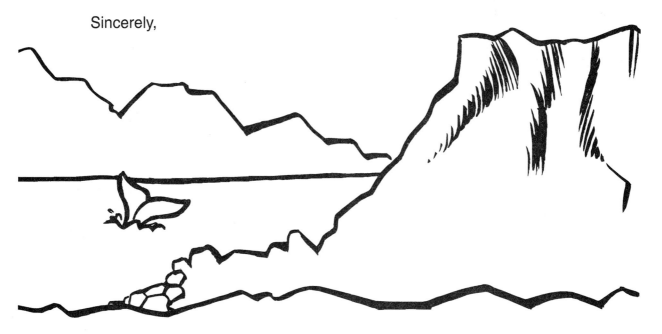

Reproducible Art

   FS123248 One-Minute Math Level B Division

Manipulative Mat

FS123248 One-Minute Math Level B Division

Game Sheet

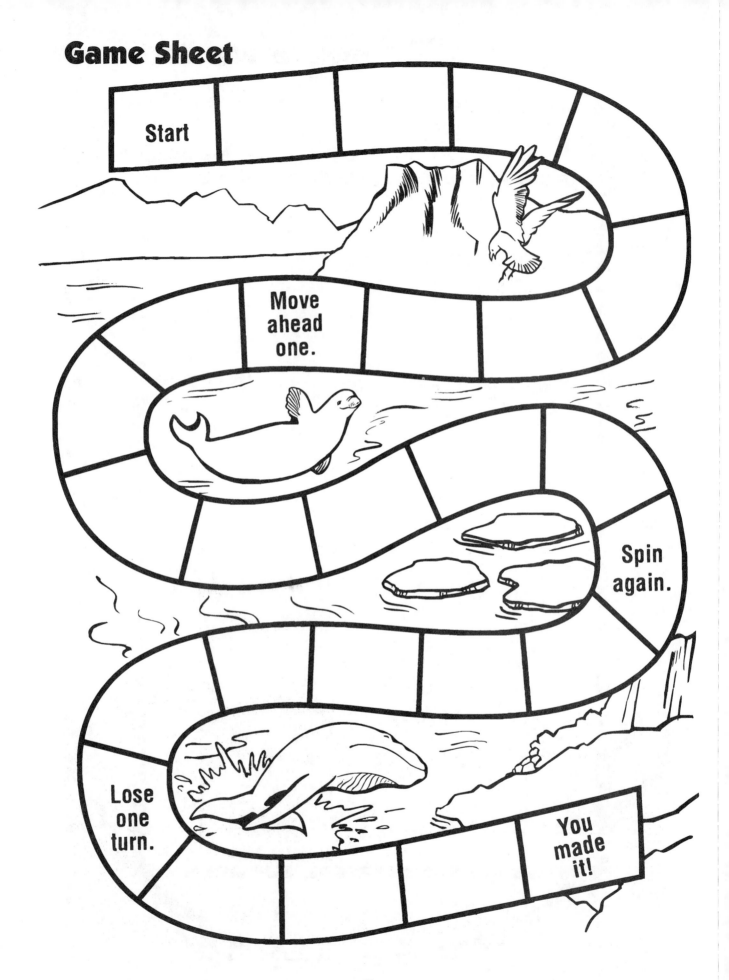

Start

Move
ahead
one.

Spin
again.

Lose
one
turn.

You
made
it!

viii   FS123248 One-Minute Math Level B Division

Congratulations!

has completed Level B Division
Divisors 6 to 9

Terrific Work!

Progress Chart **Level B Division**   **Divisors 6 to 9**

Name	Pl. Test	Pretest	6÷6	12÷6	18÷6	24÷6	30÷6	36÷6	42÷6	48÷6	54÷6	60÷6	6's Test	7÷7	14÷7	21÷7	28÷7	35÷7	42÷7	49÷7	56÷7	63÷7	70÷7	7's Test

X FS123248 One-Minute Math Level B Division

Progress Chart   Level B Division   Divisors 6 to 9

Name	8÷8	16÷8	24÷8	32÷8	40÷8	48÷8	56÷8	64÷8	72÷8	80÷8	8's Test	9÷9	18÷9	27÷9	36÷9	45÷9	54÷9	63÷9	72÷9	81÷9	90÷9	9's Test	Test

     FS123248 One-Minute Math Level B Division

Student Progress Chart

This chart belongs to _____

Color each math fact that you have learned.

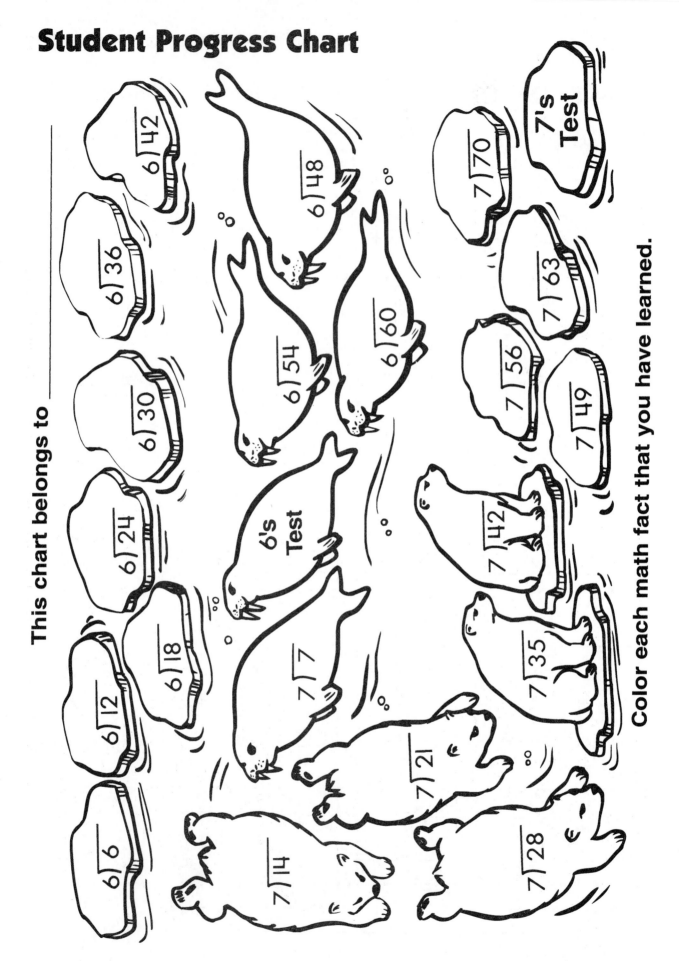

xii

Student Progress Chart

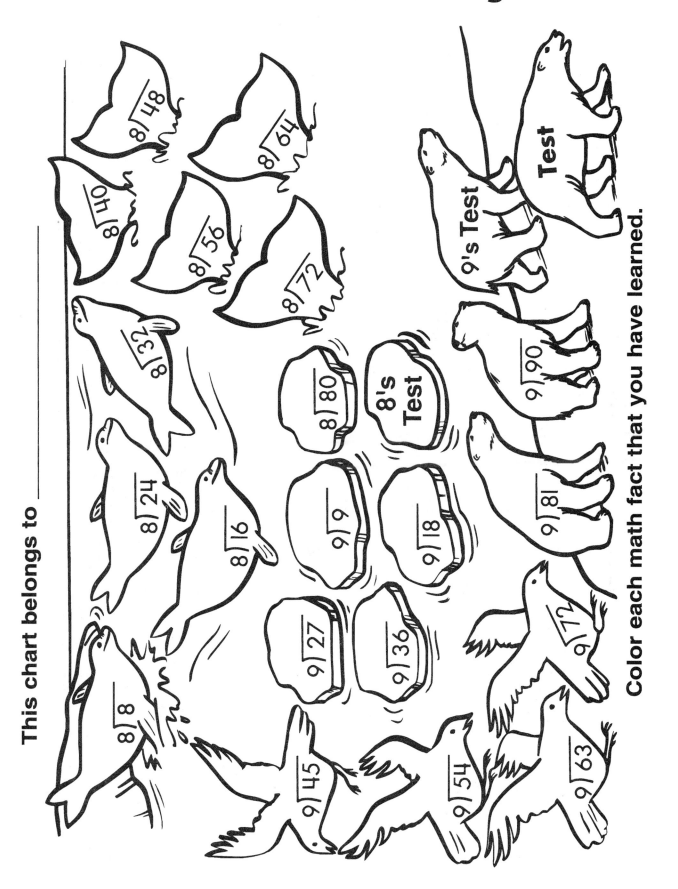

This chart belongs to _____

Color each math fact that you have learned.

$8\overline{)48}$ $8\overline{)64}$ $8\overline{)40}$ $8\overline{)56}$ $8\overline{)72}$

$8\overline{)32}$ $8\overline{)24}$ $8\overline{)16}$ $8\overline{)80}$ 8's Test

$8\overline{)8}$ $9\overline{)9}$ $9\overline{)18}$

$9\overline{)27}$ $9\overline{)36}$

$9\overline{)45}$ $9\overline{)54}$ $9\overline{)63}$

$9\overline{)72}$ $9\overline{)81}$ $9\overline{)90}$ 9's Test Test

FS123248 One-Minute Math Level B Division

Name _____

$3\overline{)21}$ $5\overline{)35}$ $4\overline{)28}$ $3\overline{)27}$ $5\overline{)30}$

$5\overline{)15}$ $4\overline{)8}$ $3\overline{)9}$ $4\overline{)36}$ $3\overline{)30}$

$4\overline{)16}$ $2\overline{)18}$ $5\overline{)50}$ $3\overline{)15}$ $4\overline{)24}$

$5\overline{)40}$ $4\overline{)32}$ $5\overline{)20}$ $4\overline{)12}$ $3\overline{)24}$

$4\overline{)4}$ $5\overline{)25}$ $3\overline{)18}$ $4\overline{)40}$ $5\overline{)45}$

$3\overline{)12}$ $4\overline{)20}$ $1\overline{)6}$ $5\overline{)10}$ $2\overline{)16}$

Name _____

$6\overline{)30}$ $7\overline{)63}$ $6\overline{)48}$ $8\overline{)32}$ $7\overline{)49}$

$7\overline{)14}$ $9\overline{)54}$ $7\overline{)28}$ $9\overline{)72}$ $8\overline{)16}$

$8\overline{)48}$ $7\overline{)35}$ $8\overline{)40}$ $6\overline{)54}$ $9\overline{)18}$

$9\overline{)63}$ $6\overline{)24}$ $8\overline{)56}$ $9\overline{)36}$ $7\overline{)42}$

$8\overline{)24}$ $7\overline{)56}$ $9\overline{)81}$ $7\overline{)21}$ $8\overline{)72}$

$9\overline{)27}$ $6\overline{)42}$ $8\overline{)64}$ $9\overline{)45}$ $6\overline{)36}$

Name _____

$4\overline{)24}$ $5\overline{)40}$ $6\overline{)6}$ $4\overline{)36}$ $6\overline{)6}$

$5\overline{)25}$ $6\overline{)6}$ $3\overline{)27}$ $6\overline{)6}$ $5\overline{)50}$

$6\overline{)6}$ $3\overline{)21}$ $6\overline{)6}$ $5\overline{)30}$ $4\overline{)20}$

$4\overline{)32}$ $6\overline{)6}$ $5\overline{)45}$ $6\overline{)6}$ $5\overline{)20}$

$6\overline{)6}$ $5\overline{)35}$ $4\overline{)28}$ $4\overline{)16}$ $6\overline{)6}$

$2\overline{)18}$ $6\overline{)6}$ $3\overline{)24}$ $6\overline{)6}$ $3\overline{)18}$

Name _____

$6\overline{)6}$ $\quad$ $4\overline{)24}$ $\quad$ $6\overline{)12}$ $\quad$ $3\overline{)21}$ $\quad$ $6\overline{)12}$

$4\overline{)32}$ $\quad$ $6\overline{)12}$ $\quad$ $6\overline{)6}$ $\quad$ $6\overline{)12}$ $\quad$ $3\overline{)27}$

$6\overline{)12}$ $\quad$ $3\overline{)9}$ $\quad$ $6\overline{)12}$ $\quad$ $4\overline{)40}$ $\quad$ $6\overline{)6}$

$3\overline{)24}$ $\quad$ $6\overline{)12}$ $\quad$ $6\overline{)6}$ $\quad$ $4\overline{)28}$ $\quad$ $6\overline{)12}$

$6\overline{)12}$ $\quad$ $3\overline{)30}$ $\quad$ $6\overline{)12}$ $\quad$ $6\overline{)6}$ $\quad$ $4\overline{)36}$

$6\overline{)6}$ $\quad$ $6\overline{)12}$ $\quad$ $4\overline{)12}$ $\quad$ $6\overline{)12}$ $\quad$ $3\overline{)15}$

$6\overline{)12}$ $5\overline{)45}$ $6\overline{)18}$ $6\overline{)6}$ $6\overline{)18}$

$3\overline{)27}$ $6\overline{)18}$ $6\overline{)12}$ $6\overline{)18}$ $4\overline{)36}$

$6\overline{)18}$ $4\overline{)24}$ $6\overline{)18}$ $6\overline{)6}$ $6\overline{)12}$

$4\overline{)32}$ $6\overline{)18}$ $6\overline{)12}$ $5\overline{)40}$ $6\overline{)18}$

$6\overline{)18}$ $6\overline{)6}$ $6\overline{)18}$ $6\overline{)12}$ $4\overline{)28}$

$6\overline{)12}$ $6\overline{)18}$ $6\overline{)0}$ $6\overline{)18}$ $3\overline{)24}$

$6\overline{)18}$ $5\overline{)50}$ $6\overline{)24}$ $6\overline{)12}$ $6\overline{)24}$

$3\overline{)21}$ $6\overline{)24}$ $6\overline{)18}$ $6\overline{)24}$ $6\overline{)6}$

$6\overline{)24}$ $6\overline{)12}$ $6\overline{)24}$ $5\overline{)35}$ $6\overline{)18}$

$6\overline{)0}$ $6\overline{)24}$ $6\overline{)18}$ $4\overline{)20}$ $6\overline{)24}$

$6\overline{)24}$ $3\overline{)18}$ $6\overline{)24}$ $6\overline{)18}$ $6\overline{)12}$

$6\overline{)18}$ $6\overline{)24}$ $5\overline{)30}$ $6\overline{)24}$ $4\overline{)16}$

$6\overline{)24}$ $4\overline{)12}$ $6\overline{)30}$ $6\overline{)18}$ $6\overline{)30}$

$5\overline{)20}$ $6\overline{)30}$ $6\overline{)24}$ $6\overline{)30}$ $6\overline{)12}$

$6\overline{)30}$ $6\overline{)18}$ $6\overline{)30}$ $5\overline{)25}$ $6\overline{)24}$

$6\overline{)12}$ $6\overline{)30}$ $6\overline{)24}$ $3\overline{)15}$ $6\overline{)30}$

$6\overline{)30}$ $6\overline{)6}$ $6\overline{)30}$ $6\overline{)24}$ $4\overline{)8}$

$6\overline{)24}$ $6\overline{)30}$ $6\overline{)18}$ $6\overline{)30}$ $3\overline{)12}$

Name _____

$6\overline{)30}$ $3\overline{)24}$ $6\overline{)36}$ $6\overline{)24}$ $6\overline{)36}$

$5\overline{)50}$ $6\overline{)36}$ $6\overline{)30}$ $6\overline{)36}$ $6\overline{)18}$

$6\overline{)36}$ $6\overline{)24}$ $6\overline{)36}$ $4\overline{)32}$ $6\overline{)30}$

$3\overline{)27}$ $6\overline{)36}$ $6\overline{)30}$ $5\overline{)45}$ $6\overline{)36}$

$6\overline{)36}$ $6\overline{)18}$ $6\overline{)36}$ $6\overline{)30}$ $6\overline{)12}$

$6\overline{)30}$ $6\overline{)36}$ $6\overline{)24}$ $6\overline{)36}$ $4\overline{)28}$

$$6\overline{)36} \quad 6\overline{)18} \quad 6\overline{)42} \quad 6\overline{)30} \quad 6\overline{)42}$$

$$5\overline{)40} \quad 6\overline{)42} \quad 6\overline{)36} \quad 6\overline{)42} \quad 6\overline{)24}$$

$$6\overline{)42} \quad 6\overline{)30} \quad 6\overline{)42} \quad 4\overline{)40} \quad 6\overline{)36}$$

$$6\overline{)12} \quad 6\overline{)42} \quad 6\overline{)36} \quad 6\overline{)24} \quad 6\overline{)42}$$

$$6\overline{)42} \quad 4\overline{)36} \quad 6\overline{)42} \quad 6\overline{)36} \quad 6\overline{)18}$$

$$6\overline{)36} \quad 6\overline{)42} \quad 6\overline{)30} \quad 6\overline{)42} \quad 6\overline{)24}$$

$6\overline{)42}$ $5\overline{)35}$ $6\overline{)48}$ $6\overline{)36}$ $6\overline{)48}$

$6\overline{)18}$ $6\overline{)48}$ $6\overline{)42}$ $6\overline{)48}$ $6\overline{)30}$

$6\overline{)48}$ $6\overline{)36}$ $6\overline{)48}$ $6\overline{)24}$ $6\overline{)42}$

$4\overline{)24}$ $6\overline{)48}$ $6\overline{)42}$ $3\overline{)21}$ $6\overline{)48}$

$6\overline{)48}$ $6\overline{)30}$ $6\overline{)48}$ $6\overline{)42}$ $6\overline{)24}$

$6\overline{)42}$ $6\overline{)48}$ $6\overline{)36}$ $6\overline{)48}$ $6\overline{)12}$

$6\overline{)48}$ $4\overline{)20}$ $6\overline{)54}$ $6\overline{)42}$ $6\overline{)54}$

$6\overline{)30}$ $6\overline{)54}$ $6\overline{)48}$ $6\overline{)54}$ $6\overline{)36}$

$6\overline{)54}$ $6\overline{)42}$ $6\overline{)54}$ $6\overline{)24}$ $6\overline{)48}$

$3\overline{)18}$ $6\overline{)54}$ $6\overline{)48}$ $6\overline{)36}$ $6\overline{)54}$

$6\overline{)54}$ $6\overline{)18}$ $6\overline{)54}$ $6\overline{)48}$ $6\overline{)30}$

$6\overline{)48}$ $6\overline{)54}$ $6\overline{)42}$ $6\overline{)54}$ $6\overline{)36}$

$6\overline{)54}$ $6\overline{)42}$ $6\overline{)60}$ $6\overline{)48}$ $6\overline{)60}$

$6\overline{)30}$ $6\overline{)60}$ $6\overline{)54}$ $6\overline{)60}$ $6\overline{)36}$

$6\overline{)60}$ $6\overline{)48}$ $6\overline{)60}$ $6\overline{)42}$ $6\overline{)54}$

$6\overline{)18}$ $6\overline{)60}$ $6\overline{)54}$ $6\overline{)12}$ $6\overline{)60}$

$6\overline{)60}$ $6\overline{)36}$ $6\overline{)60}$ $6\overline{)54}$ $6\overline{)24}$

$6\overline{)54}$ $6\overline{)60}$ $6\overline{)48}$ $6\overline{)60}$ $6\overline{)42}$

Name _____

$6\overline{)30}$ $6\overline{)54}$ $6\overline{)12}$ $6\overline{)60}$ $6\overline{)42}$

$6\overline{)0}$ $6\overline{)18}$ $6\overline{)48}$ $6\overline{)36}$ $6\overline{)6}$

$6\overline{)24}$ $6\overline{)42}$ $6\overline{)12}$ $6\overline{)54}$ $6\overline{)30}$

$6\overline{)12}$ $6\overline{)60}$ $6\overline{)36}$ $6\overline{)18}$ $6\overline{)48}$

$6\overline{)18}$ $6\overline{)30}$ $6\overline{)6}$ $6\overline{)42}$ $6\overline{)24}$

$6\overline{)54}$ $6\overline{)36}$ $6\overline{)24}$ $6\overline{)48}$ $6\overline{)60}$

$6\overline{)60}$ $6\overline{)42}$ $7\overline{)7}$ $6\overline{)54}$ $7\overline{)7}$

$6\overline{)30}$ $7\overline{)7}$ $6\overline{)60}$ $7\overline{)7}$ $6\overline{)48}$

$7\overline{)7}$ $6\overline{)54}$ $7\overline{)7}$ $6\overline{)36}$ $6\overline{)60}$

$6\overline{)48}$ $7\overline{)7}$ $6\overline{)60}$ $6\overline{)42}$ $7\overline{)7}$

$7\overline{)7}$ $6\overline{)36}$ $7\overline{)7}$ $6\overline{)60}$ $6\overline{)54}$

$6\overline{)60}$ $7\overline{)7}$ $6\overline{)54}$ $7\overline{)7}$ $6\overline{)24}$

Name _____

$$7\overline{)7} \quad 6\overline{)54} \quad 7\overline{)14} \quad 6\overline{)36} \quad 7\overline{)14}$$

$$6\overline{)42} \quad 7\overline{)14} \quad 7\overline{)7} \quad 7\overline{)14} \quad 6\overline{)60}$$

$$7\overline{)14} \quad 6\overline{)36} \quad 7\overline{)14} \quad 6\overline{)48} \quad 6\overline{)30}$$

$$6\overline{)18} \quad 7\overline{)14} \quad 7\overline{)7} \quad 6\overline{)54} \quad 7\overline{)14}$$

$$7\overline{)14} \quad 6\overline{)60} \quad 7\overline{)14} \quad 7\overline{)7} \quad 6\overline{)42}$$

$$7\overline{)7} \quad 7\overline{)14} \quad 6\overline{)48} \quad 7\overline{)14} \quad 6\overline{)24}$$

$7\overline{)14}$ $6\overline{)60}$ $7\overline{)21}$ $6\overline{)42}$ $7\overline{)21}$

$6\overline{)30}$ $7\overline{)21}$ $7\overline{)14}$ $7\overline{)21}$ $7\overline{)7}$

$7\overline{)21}$ $6\overline{)18}$ $7\overline{)21}$ $6\overline{)54}$ $7\overline{)14}$

$6\overline{)42}$ $7\overline{)21}$ $7\overline{)14}$ $6\overline{)36}$ $7\overline{)21}$

$7\overline{)21}$ $6\overline{)48}$ $7\overline{)21}$ $7\overline{)14}$ $6\overline{)24}$

$7\overline{)14}$ $7\overline{)21}$ $6\overline{)12}$ $7\overline{)21}$ $6\overline{)54}$

$7\overline{)21}$ $6\overline{)60}$ $7\overline{)28}$ $7\overline{)14}$ $7\overline{)28}$

$6\overline{)42}$ $7\overline{)28}$ $7\overline{)21}$ $7\overline{)28}$ $7\overline{)7}$

$7\overline{)28}$ $7\overline{)14}$ $7\overline{)28}$ $6\overline{)24}$ $7\overline{)21}$

$6\overline{)30}$ $7\overline{)28}$ $7\overline{)21}$ $6\overline{)54}$ $7\overline{)28}$

$7\overline{)28}$ $6\overline{)48}$ $7\overline{)28}$ $7\overline{)21}$ $6\overline{)36}$

$7\overline{)21}$ $7\overline{)28}$ $7\overline{)14}$ $7\overline{)28}$ $6\overline{)18}$

$7\overline{)28}$ $6\overline{)48}$ $7\overline{)35}$ $7\overline{)21}$ $7\overline{)35}$

$7\overline{)7}$ $7\overline{)35}$ $7\overline{)28}$ $7\overline{)35}$ $7\overline{)14}$

$7\overline{)35}$ $7\overline{)21}$ $7\overline{)35}$ $6\overline{)54}$ $7\overline{)28}$

$6\overline{)42}$ $7\overline{)35}$ $7\overline{)28}$ $6\overline{)30}$ $7\overline{)35}$

$7\overline{)35}$ $6\overline{)24}$ $7\overline{)35}$ $7\overline{)28}$ $7\overline{)21}$

$7\overline{)28}$ $7\overline{)35}$ $6\overline{)36}$ $7\overline{)35}$ $6\overline{)18}$

$$7\overline{)35} \quad 6\overline{)60} \quad 7\overline{)42} \quad 7\overline{)28} \quad 7\overline{)42}$$

$$6\overline{)42} \quad 7\overline{)42} \quad 7\overline{)35} \quad 7\overline{)42} \quad 7\overline{)21}$$

$$7\overline{)42} \quad 7\overline{)28} \quad 7\overline{)42} \quad 6\overline{)54} \quad 7\overline{)35}$$

$$6\overline{)36} \quad 7\overline{)42} \quad 7\overline{)35} \quad 7\overline{)14} \quad 7\overline{)42}$$

$$7\overline{)42} \quad 7\overline{)21} \quad 7\overline{)42} \quad 7\overline{)35} \quad 6\overline{)48}$$

$$7\overline{)35} \quad 7\overline{)42} \quad 7\overline{)28} \quad 7\overline{)42} \quad 6\overline{)30}$$

$$7\overline{)42} \qquad 7\overline{)14} \qquad 7\overline{)49} \qquad 7\overline{)35} \qquad 7\overline{)49}$$

$$6\overline{)24} \qquad 7\overline{)49} \qquad 7\overline{)42} \qquad 7\overline{)49} \qquad 7\overline{)28}$$

$$7\overline{)49} \qquad 7\overline{)35} \qquad 7\overline{)49} \qquad 7\overline{)21} \qquad 7\overline{)42}$$

$$6\overline{)12} \qquad 7\overline{)49} \qquad 7\overline{)42} \qquad 7\overline{)7} \qquad 7\overline{)49}$$

$$7\overline{)49} \qquad 7\overline{)28} \qquad 7\overline{)49} \qquad 7\overline{)42} \qquad 6\overline{)18}$$

$$7\overline{)42} \qquad 7\overline{)49} \qquad 7\overline{)35} \qquad 7\overline{)49} \qquad 7\overline{)21}$$

$7\overline{)49}$ $7\overline{)28}$ $7\overline{)56}$ $7\overline{)42}$ $7\overline{)56}$

$7\overline{)21}$ $7\overline{)56}$ $7\overline{)49}$ $7\overline{)56}$ $7\overline{)35}$

$7\overline{)56}$ $7\overline{)42}$ $7\overline{)56}$ $7\overline{)14}$ $7\overline{)49}$

$7\overline{)35}$ $7\overline{)56}$ $7\overline{)49}$ $7\overline{)28}$ $7\overline{)56}$

$7\overline{)56}$ $6\overline{)54}$ $7\overline{)56}$ $7\overline{)49}$ $7\overline{)21}$

$7\overline{)49}$ $7\overline{)56}$ $7\overline{)42}$ $7\overline{)56}$ $6\overline{)48}$

Name _____

$7\overline{)56}$ $\quad$ $7\overline{)28}$ $\quad$ $7\overline{)63}$ $\quad$ $7\overline{)49}$ $\quad$ $7\overline{)63}$

$6\overline{)36}$ $\quad$ $7\overline{)63}$ $\quad$ $7\overline{)56}$ $\quad$ $7\overline{)63}$ $\quad$ $7\overline{)42}$

$7\overline{)63}$ $\quad$ $7\overline{)49}$ $\quad$ $7\overline{)63}$ $\quad$ $7\overline{)35}$ $\quad$ $7\overline{)56}$

$6\overline{)30}$ $\quad$ $7\overline{)63}$ $\quad$ $7\overline{)56}$ $\quad$ $7\overline{)21}$ $\quad$ $7\overline{)63}$

$7\overline{)63}$ $\quad$ $7\overline{)42}$ $\quad$ $7\overline{)63}$ $\quad$ $7\overline{)56}$ $\quad$ $6\overline{)42}$

$7\overline{)56}$ $\quad$ $7\overline{)63}$ $\quad$ $7\overline{)14}$ $\quad$ $7\overline{)63}$ $\quad$ $7\overline{)49}$

$7\overline{)63}$ $7\overline{)21}$ $7\overline{)70}$ $7\overline{)56}$ $7\overline{)70}$

$7\overline{)35}$ $7\overline{)70}$ $7\overline{)63}$ $7\overline{)70}$ $7\overline{)49}$

$7\overline{)70}$ $7\overline{)56}$ $7\overline{)70}$ $6\overline{)24}$ $7\overline{)63}$

$6\overline{)18}$ $7\overline{)70}$ $7\overline{)63}$ $7\overline{)42}$ $7\overline{)70}$

$7\overline{)70}$ $7\overline{)49}$ $7\overline{)70}$ $7\overline{)63}$ $7\overline{)14}$

$7\overline{)63}$ $7\overline{)70}$ $7\overline{)28}$ $7\overline{)70}$ $7\overline{)56}$

$7\overline{)14}$ $7\overline{)63}$ $7\overline{)49}$ $7\overline{)70}$ $7\overline{)42}$

$7\overline{)28}$ $7\overline{)0}$ $7\overline{)56}$ $7\overline{)35}$ $7\overline{)21}$

$7\overline{)49}$ $7\overline{)14}$ $7\overline{)42}$ $7\overline{)63}$ $7\overline{)7}$

$7\overline{)21}$ $7\overline{)70}$ $7\overline{)35}$ $7\overline{)28}$ $7\overline{)56}$

$7\overline{)7}$ $7\overline{)42}$ $7\overline{)21}$ $7\overline{)49}$ $7\overline{)14}$

$7\overline{)63}$ $7\overline{)35}$ $7\overline{)28}$ $7\overline{)56}$ $7\overline{)70}$

Name _____

$7 \overline{)70}$ $7 \overline{)42}$ $8 \overline{)8}$ $7 \overline{)63}$ $8 \overline{)8}$

$6 \overline{)60}$ $8 \overline{)8}$ $7 \overline{)70}$ $8 \overline{)8}$ $7 \overline{)56}$

$8 \overline{)8}$ $7 \overline{)63}$ $8 \overline{)8}$ $7 \overline{)49}$ $7 \overline{)70}$

$6 \overline{)54}$ $8 \overline{)8}$ $7 \overline{)70}$ $7 \overline{)35}$ $8 \overline{)8}$

$8 \overline{)8}$ $7 \overline{)56}$ $8 \overline{)8}$ $7 \overline{)70}$ $7 \overline{)21}$

$7 \overline{)70}$ $8 \overline{)8}$ $7 \overline{)28}$ $8 \overline{)8}$ $7 \overline{)63}$

$$8\overline{)8} \qquad 7\overline{)49} \qquad 8\overline{)16} \qquad 7\overline{)70} \qquad 8\overline{)16}$$

$$7\overline{)56} \qquad 8\overline{)16} \qquad 8\overline{)8} \qquad 8\overline{)16} \qquad 7\overline{)63}$$

$$8\overline{)16} \qquad 7\overline{)70} \qquad 8\overline{)16} \qquad 7\overline{)42} \qquad 8\overline{)8}$$

$$7\overline{)35} \qquad 8\overline{)16} \qquad 8\overline{)8} \qquad 7\overline{)56} \qquad 8\overline{)16}$$

$$8\overline{)16} \qquad 7\overline{)63} \qquad 8\overline{)16} \qquad 8\overline{)8} \qquad 7\overline{)21}$$

$$8\overline{)8} \qquad 8\overline{)16} \qquad 7\overline{)28} \qquad 8\overline{)16} \qquad 7\overline{)70}$$

$8\overline{)16}$ $7\overline{)35}$ $8\overline{)24}$ $7\overline{)49}$ $8\overline{)24}$

$7\overline{)63}$ $8\overline{)24}$ $8\overline{)16}$ $8\overline{)24}$ $8\overline{)8}$

$8\overline{)24}$ $7\overline{)42}$ $8\overline{)24}$ $7\overline{)14}$ $8\overline{)16}$

$7\overline{)56}$ $8\overline{)24}$ $8\overline{)16}$ $7\overline{)70}$ $8\overline{)24}$

$8\overline{)24}$ $7\overline{)28}$ $8\overline{)24}$ $8\overline{)16}$ $6\overline{)54}$

$8\overline{)16}$ $8\overline{)24}$ $6\overline{)48}$ $8\overline{)24}$ $7\overline{)21}$

$8\overline{)24}$ $7\overline{)56}$ $8\overline{)32}$ $8\overline{)16}$ $8\overline{)32}$

$7\overline{)70}$ $8\overline{)32}$ $8\overline{)24}$ $8\overline{)32}$ $7\overline{)42}$

$8\overline{)32}$ $8\overline{)16}$ $8\overline{)32}$ $6\overline{)42}$ $8\overline{)24}$

$7\overline{)35}$ $8\overline{)32}$ $8\overline{)24}$ $7\overline{)63}$ $8\overline{)32}$

$8\overline{)32}$ $7\overline{)49}$ $8\overline{)32}$ $8\overline{)24}$ $8\overline{)16}$

$8\overline{)24}$ $8\overline{)32}$ $7\overline{)28}$ $8\overline{)32}$ $7\overline{)21}$

Name _____

$8\overline{)32}$ $\quad$ $7\overline{)42}$ $\quad$ $8\overline{)40}$ $\quad$ $8\overline{)24}$ $\quad$ $8\overline{)40}$

$7\overline{)56}$ $\quad$ $8\overline{)40}$ $\quad$ $8\overline{)32}$ $\quad$ $8\overline{)40}$ $\quad$ $8\overline{)16}$

$8\overline{)40}$ $\quad$ $8\overline{)24}$ $\quad$ $8\overline{)40}$ $\quad$ $7\overline{)63}$ $\quad$ $8\overline{)32}$

$6\overline{)36}$ $\quad$ $8\overline{)40}$ $\quad$ $8\overline{)32}$ $\quad$ $8\overline{)8}$ $\quad$ $8\overline{)40}$

$8\overline{)40}$ $\quad$ $8\overline{)16}$ $\quad$ $8\overline{)40}$ $\quad$ $8\overline{)32}$ $\quad$ $7\overline{)70}$

$8\overline{)32}$ $\quad$ $8\overline{)40}$ $\quad$ $7\overline{)49}$ $\quad$ $8\overline{)40}$ $\quad$ $8\overline{)24}$

Name _____

$8\overline{)40}$ $6\overline{)36}$ $8\overline{)48}$ $8\overline{)32}$ $8\overline{)48}$

$7\overline{)70}$ $8\overline{)48}$ $8\overline{)40}$ $8\overline{)48}$ $8\overline{)24}$

$8\overline{)48}$ $8\overline{)32}$ $8\overline{)48}$ $8\overline{)16}$ $8\overline{)40}$

$7\overline{)56}$ $8\overline{)48}$ $8\overline{)40}$ $7\overline{)63}$ $8\overline{)48}$

$8\overline{)48}$ $8\overline{)24}$ $8\overline{)48}$ $8\overline{)40}$ $7\overline{)42}$

$8\overline{)40}$ $8\overline{)48}$ $7\overline{)49}$ $8\overline{)48}$ $8\overline{)32}$

$$8\overline{)48} \qquad 6\overline{)30} \qquad 8\overline{)56} \qquad 8\overline{)40} \qquad 8\overline{)56}$$

$$7\overline{)49} \qquad 8\overline{)56} \qquad 8\overline{)48} \qquad 8\overline{)56} \qquad 8\overline{)32}$$

$$8\overline{)56} \qquad 8\overline{)40} \qquad 8\overline{)56} \qquad 8\overline{)24} \qquad 8\overline{)48}$$

$$8\overline{)16} \qquad 8\overline{)56} \qquad 8\overline{)48} \qquad 7\overline{)63} \qquad 8\overline{)56}$$

$$8\overline{)56} \qquad 8\overline{)32} \qquad 8\overline{)56} \qquad 8\overline{)48} \qquad 7\overline{)56}$$

$$8\overline{)48} \qquad 8\overline{)56} \qquad 8\overline{)24} \qquad 8\overline{)56} \qquad 8\overline{)40}$$

Name _____

$8\overline{)56}$ $6\overline{)18}$ $8\overline{)64}$ $8\overline{)48}$ $8\overline{)64}$

$8\overline{)24}$ $8\overline{)64}$ $8\overline{)56}$ $8\overline{)64}$ $7\overline{)42}$

$8\overline{)64}$ $8\overline{)48}$ $8\overline{)64}$ $8\overline{)40}$ $8\overline{)56}$

$6\overline{)24}$ $8\overline{)64}$ $8\overline{)56}$ $8\overline{)16}$ $8\overline{)64}$

$8\overline{)64}$ $7\overline{)35}$ $8\overline{)64}$ $8\overline{)56}$ $8\overline{)32}$

$8\overline{)56}$ $8\overline{)64}$ $8\overline{)40}$ $8\overline{)64}$ $8\overline{)48}$

$8\overline{)64}$ $8\overline{)32}$ $8\overline{)72}$ $8\overline{)56}$ $8\overline{)72}$

$7\overline{)28}$ $8\overline{)72}$ $8\overline{)64}$ $8\overline{)72}$ $8\overline{)48}$

$8\overline{)72}$ $8\overline{)56}$ $8\overline{)72}$ $8\overline{)40}$ $8\overline{)64}$

$8\overline{)16}$ $8\overline{)72}$ $8\overline{)64}$ $8\overline{)24}$ $8\overline{)72}$

$8\overline{)72}$ $8\overline{)48}$ $8\overline{)72}$ $8\overline{)64}$ $7\overline{)21}$

$8\overline{)64}$ $8\overline{)72}$ $6\overline{)60}$ $8\overline{)72}$ $8\overline{)56}$

Name _____

$8\overline{)72}$ $7\overline{)63}$ $8\overline{)80}$ $8\overline{)64}$ $8\overline{)80}$

$8\overline{)56}$ $8\overline{)80}$ $8\overline{)72}$ $8\overline{)80}$ $8\overline{)32}$

$8\overline{)80}$ $8\overline{)64}$ $8\overline{)80}$ $8\overline{)48}$ $8\overline{)72}$

$8\overline{)40}$ $8\overline{)80}$ $8\overline{)72}$ $8\overline{)24}$ $8\overline{)80}$

$8\overline{)80}$ $6\overline{)54}$ $8\overline{)80}$ $8\overline{)72}$ $8\overline{)56}$

$8\overline{)72}$ $8\overline{)80}$ $8\overline{)16}$ $8\overline{)80}$ $8\overline{)64}$

$8\overline{)64}$ $8\overline{)32}$ $8\overline{)40}$ $8\overline{)80}$ $8\overline{)8}$

$8\overline{)24}$ $8\overline{)72}$ $8\overline{)56}$ $8\overline{)16}$ $8\overline{)48}$

$8\overline{)16}$ $8\overline{)40}$ $8\overline{)0}$ $8\overline{)64}$ $8\overline{)32}$

$8\overline{)56}$ $8\overline{)80}$ $8\overline{)48}$ $8\overline{)24}$ $8\overline{)72}$

$8\overline{)32}$ $8\overline{)8}$ $8\overline{)40}$ $8\overline{)56}$ $8\overline{)16}$

$8\overline{)72}$ $8\overline{)24}$ $8\overline{)64}$ $8\overline{)48}$ $8\overline{)80}$

$8\overline{)80}$ $8\overline{)40}$ $9\overline{)9}$ $8\overline{)72}$ $9\overline{)9}$

$6\overline{)48}$ $9\overline{)9}$ $8\overline{)80}$ $9\overline{)9}$ $8\overline{)64}$

$9\overline{)9}$ $8\overline{)72}$ $9\overline{)9}$ $8\overline{)56}$ $8\overline{)80}$

$8\overline{)48}$ $9\overline{)9}$ $8\overline{)80}$ $8\overline{)32}$ $9\overline{)9}$

$9\overline{)9}$ $8\overline{)64}$ $9\overline{)9}$ $8\overline{)80}$ $7\overline{)56}$

$8\overline{)80}$ $9\overline{)9}$ $8\overline{)56}$ $9\overline{)9}$ $8\overline{)72}$

$9\overline{)9}$ $8\overline{)64}$ $9\overline{)18}$ $8\overline{)80}$ $9\overline{)18}$

$8\overline{)56}$ $9\overline{)18}$ $9\overline{)9}$ $9\overline{)18}$ $8\overline{)72}$

$9\overline{)18}$ $8\overline{)80}$ $9\overline{)18}$ $8\overline{)40}$ $9\overline{)9}$

$7\overline{)49}$ $9\overline{)18}$ $9\overline{)9}$ $8\overline{)64}$ $9\overline{)18}$

$9\overline{)18}$ $8\overline{)72}$ $9\overline{)18}$ $9\overline{)9}$ $8\overline{)48}$

$9\overline{)9}$ $9\overline{)18}$ $6\overline{)42}$ $9\overline{)18}$ $8\overline{)80}$

Name _____

$9\overline{)18}$ $8\overline{)56}$ $9\overline{)27}$ $9\overline{)9}$ $9\overline{)27}$

$8\overline{)72}$ $9\overline{)27}$ $9\overline{)18}$ $9\overline{)27}$ $8\overline{)80}$

$9\overline{)27}$ $8\overline{)40}$ $9\overline{)27}$ $8\overline{)64}$ $9\overline{)18}$

$7\overline{)42}$ $9\overline{)27}$ $9\overline{)18}$ $8\overline{)48}$ $9\overline{)27}$

$9\overline{)27}$ $9\overline{)9}$ $9\overline{)27}$ $9\overline{)18}$ $8\overline{)72}$

$9\overline{)18}$ $9\overline{)27}$ $8\overline{)64}$ $9\overline{)27}$ $6\overline{)36}$

38

$$9\overline{)27} \quad 8\overline{)64} \quad 9\overline{)36} \quad 9\overline{)18} \quad 9\overline{)36}$$

$$7\overline{)35} \quad 9\overline{)36} \quad 9\overline{)27} \quad 9\overline{)36} \quad 8\overline{)80}$$

$$9\overline{)36} \quad 9\overline{)18} \quad 9\overline{)36} \quad 9\overline{)9} \quad 9\overline{)27}$$

$$8\overline{)32} \quad 9\overline{)36} \quad 9\overline{)27} \quad 8\overline{)72} \quad 9\overline{)36}$$

$$9\overline{)36} \quad 8\overline{)48} \quad 9\overline{)36} \quad 9\overline{)27} \quad 8\overline{)56}$$

$$9\overline{)27} \quad 9\overline{)36} \quad 6\overline{)30} \quad 9\overline{)36} \quad 9\overline{)18}$$

Name _____

$9\overline{)36}$ $8\overline{)72}$ $9\overline{)45}$ $9\overline{)27}$ $9\overline{)45}$

$8\overline{)48}$ $9\overline{)45}$ $9\overline{)36}$ $9\overline{)45}$ $9\overline{)18}$

$9\overline{)45}$ $9\overline{)27}$ $9\overline{)45}$ $8\overline{)80}$ $9\overline{)36}$

$8\overline{)56}$ $9\overline{)45}$ $9\overline{)36}$ $8\overline{)64}$ $9\overline{)45}$

$9\overline{)45}$ $9\overline{)18}$ $9\overline{)45}$ $9\overline{)36}$ $6\overline{)24}$

$9\overline{)36}$ $9\overline{)45}$ $7\overline{)28}$ $9\overline{)45}$ $9\overline{)27}$

$9\overline{)45}$ $7\overline{)21}$ $9\overline{)54}$ $9\overline{)36}$ $9\overline{)54}$

$8\overline{)40}$ $9\overline{)54}$ $9\overline{)45}$ $9\overline{)54}$ $9\overline{)27}$

$9\overline{)54}$ $9\overline{)36}$ $9\overline{)54}$ $8\overline{)24}$ $9\overline{)45}$

$6\overline{)18}$ $9\overline{)54}$ $9\overline{)45}$ $9\overline{)18}$ $9\overline{)54}$

$9\overline{)54}$ $9\overline{)27}$ $9\overline{)54}$ $9\overline{)45}$ $8\overline{)32}$

$9\overline{)45}$ $9\overline{)54}$ $8\overline{)16}$ $9\overline{)54}$ $9\overline{)36}$

$9\overline{)54}$ $8\overline{)80}$ $9\overline{)63}$ $9\overline{)45}$ $9\overline{)63}$

$8\overline{)64}$ $9\overline{)63}$ $9\overline{)54}$ $9\overline{)63}$ $9\overline{)36}$

$9\overline{)63}$ $9\overline{)45}$ $9\overline{)63}$ $9\overline{)27}$ $9\overline{)54}$

$6\overline{)54}$ $9\overline{)63}$ $9\overline{)54}$ $8\overline{)72}$ $9\overline{)63}$

$9\overline{)63}$ $9\overline{)36}$ $9\overline{)63}$ $9\overline{)54}$ $7\overline{)63}$

$9\overline{)54}$ $9\overline{)63}$ $9\overline{)18}$ $9\overline{)63}$ $9\overline{)45}$

9)63	9)27	9)72	9)54	9)72
8)56	9)72	9)63	9)72	9)45
9)72	9)54	9)72	9)9	9)63
9)18	9)72	9)63	9)36	9)72
9)72	9)45	9)72	9)63	7)56
9)63	9)72	6)48	9)72	9)54

Name _____

$9\overline{)72}$ $9\overline{)45}$ $9\overline{)81}$ $9\overline{)63}$ $9\overline{)81}$

$8\overline{)48}$ $9\overline{)81}$ $9\overline{)72}$ $9\overline{)81}$ $9\overline{)54}$

$9\overline{)81}$ $9\overline{)63}$ $9\overline{)81}$ $9\overline{)18}$ $9\overline{)72}$

$9\overline{)36}$ $9\overline{)81}$ $9\overline{)72}$ $9\overline{)45}$ $9\overline{)81}$

$9\overline{)81}$ $9\overline{)54}$ $9\overline{)81}$ $9\overline{)72}$ $9\overline{)27}$

$9\overline{)72}$ $9\overline{)81}$ $7\overline{)49}$ $9\overline{)81}$ $9\overline{)63}$

$9\overline{)81}$ $9\overline{)18}$ $9\overline{)90}$ $9\overline{)72}$ $9\overline{)90}$

$6\overline{)42}$ $9\overline{)90}$ $9\overline{)81}$ $9\overline{)90}$ $9\overline{)63}$

$9\overline{)90}$ $9\overline{)72}$ $9\overline{)90}$ $9\overline{)45}$ $9\overline{)81}$

$9\overline{)27}$ $9\overline{)90}$ $9\overline{)81}$ $9\overline{)54}$ $9\overline{)90}$

$9\overline{)90}$ $9\overline{)63}$ $9\overline{)90}$ $9\overline{)81}$ $9\overline{)36}$

$9\overline{)81}$ $9\overline{)90}$ $9\overline{)54}$ $9\overline{)90}$ $9\overline{)72}$

$9\overline{)27}$ $9\overline{)81}$ $9\overline{)54}$ $9\overline{)72}$ $9\overline{)45}$

$9\overline{)18}$ $9\overline{)63}$ $9\overline{)9}$ $9\overline{)90}$ $9\overline{)36}$

$9\overline{)54}$ $9\overline{)27}$ $9\overline{)81}$ $9\overline{)45}$ $9\overline{)0}$

$9\overline{)36}$ $9\overline{)90}$ $9\overline{)18}$ $9\overline{)63}$ $9\overline{)72}$

$9\overline{)63}$ $9\overline{)45}$ $9\overline{)27}$ $9\overline{)54}$ $9\overline{)9}$

$9\overline{)81}$ $9\overline{)18}$ $9\overline{)72}$ $9\overline{)36}$ $9\overline{)90}$

$$6\overline{)36} \quad 9\overline{)45} \quad 8\overline{)64} \quad 6\overline{)42} \quad 9\overline{)27}$$

$$8\overline{)72} \quad 7\overline{)21} \quad 9\overline{)81} \quad 7\overline{)56} \quad 8\overline{)24}$$

$$7\overline{)42} \quad 9\overline{)36} \quad 8\overline{)56} \quad 6\overline{)24} \quad 9\overline{)63}$$

$$9\overline{)18} \quad 6\overline{)54} \quad 8\overline{)40} \quad 7\overline{)35} \quad 8\overline{)48}$$

$$8\overline{)16} \quad 9\overline{)72} \quad 7\overline{)28} \quad 9\overline{)54} \quad 7\overline{)14}$$

$$7\overline{)49} \quad 8\overline{)32} \quad 6\overline{)48} \quad 7\overline{)63} \quad 6\overline{)30}$$

Answer Key
Level B Division

Page one (Placement test)

7	7	7	9	6
3	2	3	9	10
4	9	10	5	6
8	8	4	3	8
1	5	6	10	9
4	5	6	2	8

Page two (Pretest)

5	9	8	4	7
2	6	4	8	2
6	5	5	9	2
7	4	7	4	6
3	8	9	3	9
3	7	8	5	6

Page three (6÷6)

6	8	1	9	1
5	1	9	1	10
1	7	1	6	5
8	1	9	1	4
1	7	7	4	1
9	1	8	1	6

Page four (12÷6)

1	6	2	7	2
8	2	1	2	9
2	3	2	10	1
8	2	1	7	2
2	10	2	1	9
1	2	3	2	5

Page five (18÷6)

2	9	3	1	3
9	3	2	3	9
3	6	3	1	2
8	3	2	8	3
3	1	3	2	7
2	3	0	3	8

Page six (24÷6)

3	10	4	2	4
7	4	3	4	1
4	2	4	7	3
0	4	3	5	4
4	6	4	3	2
3	4	6	4	4

Page seven (30÷6)

4	3	5	3	5
4	5	4	5	2
5	3	5	5	4
2	5	4	5	5
5	1	5	4	2
4	5	3	5	4

Page eight (36÷6)

5	8	6	4	6
10	6	5	6	3
6	4	6	8	5
9	6	5	9	6
6	3	6	5	2
5	6	4	6	7

Page nine (42÷6)

6	3	7	5	7
8	7	6	7	4
7	5	7	10	6
2	7	6	4	7
7	9	7	6	3
6	7	5	7	4

Page ten (48÷6)

7	7	8	6	8
3	8	7	8	5
8	6	8	4	7
6	8	7	7	8
8	5	8	7	4
7	8	6	8	2

Page eleven (54÷6)

8	5	9	7	9
5	9	8	9	6
9	7	9	4	8
6	9	8	6	9
9	3	9	8	5
8	9	7	9	6

Page twelve (60÷6)

9	7	10	8	10
5	10	9	10	6
10	8	10	7	9
3	10	9	2	10
10	6	10	9	4
9	10	8	10	7

Page thirteen (6's test)

5	9	2	10	7
0	3	8	6	1
4	7	2	9	5
2	10	6	3	8
3	5	1	7	4
9	6	4	8	10

Page fourteen (7÷7)

10	7	1	9	1
5	1	10	1	8
1	9	1	6	10
8	1	10	7	1
1	6	1	10	9
10	1	9	1	4

Page fifteen (14÷7)

1	9	2	6	2
7	2	1	2	10
2	6	2	8	5
3	2	1	9	2
2	10	2	1	7
1	2	8	2	4

Answer Key
Level B Division

Page sixteen (21÷7)

2	10	3	7	3
5	3	2	3	1
3	3	3	9	2
7	3	2	6	3
3	8	3	2	4
2	3	2	3	9

Page seventeen (28÷7)

3	10	4	2	4
7	4	3	4	1
4	2	4	4	3
5	4	3	9	4
4	8	4	3	6
3	4	2	4	3

Page eighteen (35÷7)

4	8	5	3	5
1	5	4	5	2
5	3	5	9	4
7	5	4	5	5
5	4	5	4	3
4	5	6	5	3

Page nineteen (42÷7)

5	10	6	4	6
7	6	5	6	3
6	4	6	9	5
6	6	5	2	6
6	3	6	5	8
5	6	4	6	5

Page twenty (49÷7)

6	2	7	5	7
4	7	6	7	4
7	5	7	3	6
2	7	6	1	7
7	4	7	6	3
6	7	5	7	3

Page twenty-one (56÷7)

7	4	8	6	8
3	8	7	8	5
8	6	8	2	7
5	8	7	4	8
8	9	8	7	3
7	8	6	8	8

Page twenty-two (63÷7)

8	4	9	7	9
6	9	8	9	6
9	7	9	5	8
5	9	8	3	9
9	6	9	8	7
8	9	2	9	7

Page twenty-three (70÷7)

9	3	10	8	10
5	10	9	10	7
10	8	10	4	9
3	10	9	6	10
10	7	10	9	2
9	10	4	10	8

Page twenty-four (7's test)

2	9	7	10	6
4	0	8	5	3
7	2	6	9	1
3	10	5	4	8
1	6	3	7	2
9	5	4	8	10

Page twenty-five (8÷8)

10	6	1	9	1
10	1	10	1	8
1	9	1	7	10
9	1	10	5	1
1	8	1	10	3
10	1	4	1	9

Page twenty-six (16÷8)

1	7	2	10	2
8	2	1	2	9
2	10	2	6	1
5	2	1	8	2
2	9	2	1	3
1	2	4	2	10

Page twenty-seven (24÷8)

2	5	3	7	3
9	3	2	3	1
3	6	3	2	2
8	3	2	10	3
3	4	3	2	9
2	3	8	3	3

Page twenty-eight (32÷8)

3	8	4	2	4
10	4	3	4	6
4	2	4	7	3
5	4	3	9	4
4	7	4	3	2
3	4	4	4	3

Page twenty-nine (40÷8)

4	6	5	3	5
8	5	4	5	2
5	3	5	9	4
6	5	4	1	5
5	2	5	4	10
4	5	7	5	3

Page thirty (48÷8)

5	6	6	4	6
10	6	5	6	3
6	4	6	2	5
8	6	5	9	6
6	3	6	5	6
5	6	7	6	4

49

FS123248 One-Minute Math Level B Division

Answer Key
Level B Division

Page thirty-one (56÷8)

6	5	7	5	7
7	7	6	7	4
7	5	7	3	6
2	7	6	9	7
7	4	7	6	8
6	7	3	7	5

Page thirty-two (64÷8)

7	3	8	6	8
3	8	7	8	6
8	6	8	5	7
4	8	7	2	8
8	5	8	7	4
7	8	5	8	6

Page thirty-three (72÷8)

8	4	9	7	9
4	9	8	9	6
9	7	9	5	8
2	9	8	3	9
9	6	9	8	3
8	9	10	9	7

Page thirty-four (80÷8)

9	9	10	8	10
7	10	9	10	4
10	8	10	6	9
5	10	9	3	10
10	9	10	9	7
9	10	2	10	8

Page thirty-five (8's test)

8	4	5	10	1
3	9	7	2	6
2	5	0	8	4
7	10	6	3	9
4	1	5	7	2
9	3	8	6	10

Page thirty-six (9÷9)

10	5	1	9	1
8	1	10	1	8
1	9	1	7	10
6	1	10	4	1
1	8	1	10	8
10	1	7	1	9

Page thirty-seven (18÷9)

1	8	2	10	2
7	2	1	2	9
2	10	2	5	1
7	2	1	8	2
2	9	2	1	6
1	2	7	2	10

Page thirty-eight (27÷9)

2	7	3	1	3
9	3	2	3	10
3	5	3	8	2
6	3	2	6	3
3	1	3	2	9
2	3	8	3	6

Page thirty-nine (36÷9)

3	8	4	2	4
5	4	3	4	10
4	2	4	1	3
4	4	3	9	4
4	6	4	3	7
3	4	5	4	2

Page forty (45÷9)

4	9	5	3	5
6	5	4	5	2
5	3	5	10	4
7	5	4	8	5
5	2	5	4	4
4	5	4	5	3

Page forty-one (54÷9)

5	3	6	4	6
5	6	5	6	3
6	4	6	3	5
3	6	5	2	6
6	3	6	5	4
5	6	2	6	4

Page forty-two (63÷9)

6	10	7	5	7
8	7	6	7	4
7	5	7	3	6
9	7	6	9	7
7	4	7	6	9
6	7	2	7	5

Page forty-three (72÷9)

7	3	8	6	8
7	8	7	8	5
8	6	8	1	7
2	8	7	4	8
8	5	8	7	8
7	8	8	8	6

Page forty-four (81÷9)

8	5	9	7	9
6	9	8	9	6
9	7	9	2	8
4	9	8	5	9
9	6	9	8	3
8	9	7	9	7

Page forty-five (90÷9)

9	2	10	8	10
7	10	9	10	7
10	8	10	5	9
3	10	9	6	10
10	7	10	9	4
9	10	6	10	8

Answer Key
Level B Division

Page forty-six (9's test)				
3	9	6	8	5
2	7	1	10	4
6	3	9	5	0
4	10	2	7	8
7	5	3	6	1
9	2	8	4	10

Page forty-seven (Posttest)				
6	5	8	7	3
9	3	9	8	3
6	4	7	4	7
2	9	5	5	6
2	8	4	6	2
7	4	8	9	5

FS123248 One-Minute Math Level B Division

$6 \overline{)6}$ $6 \overline{)12}$ $6 \overline{)18}$

$6 \overline{)24}$ $6 \overline{)30}$ $6 \overline{)36}$

$6 \overline{)42}$ $6 \overline{)48}$ $6 \overline{)54}$

$6 \overline{)60}$ $7 \overline{)7}$ $7 \overline{)14}$

$7 \overline{)21}$ $7 \overline{)28}$ $7 \overline{)35}$

$7 \overline{)42}$ $7 \overline{)49}$ $7 \overline{)56}$

3

2

1

6

5

4

9

8

7

2

1

10

5

4

3

8

7

6

$11\overline{)55}$ $11\overline{)66}$ $11\overline{)77}$

$11\overline{)88}$ $11\overline{)99}$ $11\overline{)110}$

$12\overline{)12}$ $12\overline{)24}$ $12\overline{)36}$

$12\overline{)48}$ $12\overline{)60}$ $12\overline{)72}$

$12\overline{)84}$ $12\overline{)96}$ $12\overline{)120}$

$12\overline{)108}$

7

6

5

10

9

8

3

2

1

6

5

4

10

8

7

9

$7\overline{)63}$ $\qquad$ $7\overline{)70}$ $\qquad$ $8\overline{)8}$

$8\overline{)16}$ $\qquad$ $8\overline{)24}$ $\qquad$ $8\overline{)32}$

$8\overline{)40}$ $\qquad$ $8\overline{)48}$ $\qquad$ $8\overline{)56}$

$8\overline{)64}$ $\qquad$ $8\overline{)72}$ $\qquad$ $8\overline{)80}$

$9\overline{)9}$ $\qquad$ $9\overline{)18}$ $\qquad$ $9\overline{)27}$

$9\overline{)36}$ $\qquad$ $9\overline{)45}$ $\qquad$ $9\overline{)54}$

1

10

9

4

3

2

7

6

5

10

9

8

3

2

1

6

5

4

$9\overline{)63}$ $9\overline{)72}$ $9\overline{)81}$

$9\overline{)90}$ $10\overline{)10}$ $10\overline{)20}$

$10\overline{)30}$ $10\overline{)40}$ $10\overline{)50}$

$10\overline{)60}$ $10\overline{)70}$ $10\overline{)80}$

$10\overline{)90}$ $10\overline{)100}$ $11\overline{)11}$

$11\overline{)22}$ $11\overline{)33}$ $11\overline{)44}$

9

8

7

2

1

10

5

4

3

8

7

6

1

10

9

4

3

2